HONOR GOD
WITH YOUR LIFE

Tiffany Purifoy

Honor God With Your Life

Copyright © 2021 Tiffany Purifoy

Scripture quotations marked (KJV) are taken from the King James Version of the Bible, public domain.

Scripture quotations marked (AMP) are taken from the Amplified Bible, copyright © 1954, 1958, 1962, 1964, 1965, 1987 by The Lockman Foundation Used by permission." (www.Lockman.org)

Scripture quotations marked (NLT) are taken from the Holy Bible, New Living Translation, copyright 1996, 2004, 2007 by Tyndale House Foundation. Used by permission of Tyndale House Publishers, Inc., Carol Stream, Illinois 60188. All rights reserved.

Scripture quotations marked (MSG) are taken from THE MESSAGE, copyright © 1993, 2002, 2018 by Eugene H. Peterson. Used by permission of NavPress. All rights reserved. Represented by Tyndale House Publishers, Inc.
Scripture quotations marked (NKJV) are taken from the New King James Version®. Copyright © 1982 by Thomas Nelson. Used by permission. All rights reserved.

Scripture quotations marked (TLB) are taken from The Living Bible copyright © 1971. Used by permission of Tyndale House Publishers, Inc., Carol Stream, Illinois 60188. All rights reserved.   ISBN: 978-1-731-34856-2

Contents

DEDICATION

I would like to dedicate this book to my family and friends. I love you dearly! Thank you all very much for your unconditional love and support.

CHAPTER 1

Embrace God's Plan

"And we know that all things work together for good to them that love God, to them who are the called according to his purpose."

–Romans 8:28 KJV

It was a day like no other. Everything that could oppose me did so to the maximum extent. By five o'clock that afternoon, I knew what I had to do. I needed to take a nice long walk and talk with the Lord about the challenges I had been facing.

There is something special about these kinds of walks. Initially, I intend to clear my mind while experiencing the beauty and peace of nature. By the time the walk is over, however, I end up with new insights that could only come from heaven.

On this nature walk, God spoke to my heart about the purposes and plans He has for our lives. As I walked along the path, I observed captivating scenes that inspired me to reflect on the idea of growth and change. The Lord reminded me of His Word in Matthew 6:28 (NLT): "Look at the lilies of the field and how they grow. They don't work or make their clothing, yet Solomon, in all his glory, was not dressed as beautifully as they are. And if God cares so wonderfully for wildflowers that are here today and thrown into the fire tomorrow, He will certainly care for you."

Like all of God's creation, we encounter sunshine and rain, but sometimes we forget to make the best of every experience, including the difficult ones. We appreciate sunny days when everything is going well. The rainy days are not so pleasant. The resistance, trouble, and bad news can be a bit overwhelming. Yet, every challenge presents an opportunity for us to see God working.

As I continued walking, I observed the trees and remembered God's promise for those who delight in His Word: "They are like trees along a riverbank bearing luscious fruit each season without fail. Their leaves shall never wither, and all they do shall prosper," (Psalm 1:3, TLB).

Notice how trees adjust to every changing season. Some trees present the most beautiful display of autumn colors during the fall, but they seem to have no life at all by winter. Yet even while their appearance is dry and brittle, their leaves fall to the ground and feed their roots, providing continuous nourishment. When spring returns, the trees bloom once again, bearing fruit and showing off their splendor.

Every season we encounter has a purpose that is ultimately for our good. God's Word gives us the nourishment we need to continue being resilient. If we respond to change by consistently focusing on God's promises despite what is happening around us, we will prosper.

Our experiences, good or bad, somehow fit into a plan God has already designed. As our Creator, He knows what we need to succeed. He knows how long we need to experience different seasons in our lives, and He knows when it is time for a change.

By the end of my walk that day, I had indescribable peace about my circumstances. The beauty surrounding me served as a reminder that God's way is perfect, and so is His plan for us. He tells us in Jeremiah 29:11 (MSG), "I know what I'm doing. I have it all planned out—plans to take care of you, not abandon you, plans to give you the future you hope for."

You Have Been Chosen

When I was a child, I always enjoyed playing neighborhood sports with my friends. We usually formed two or more teams and allowed the group's oldest members to be the captains. The most exciting part of creating teams was waiting to be chosen. When we heard our names, it meant someone felt we would make a great addition to their team. That is how God feels about you-you are especially valuable to Him, and He wants you on His team.

Many of us struggle to believe this because of the unfavorable circumstances that cause us to underestimate our worth. For this reason, some people try to overcompensate by going to great lengths to achieve significant accomplishments in hopes of finding real meaning. Yet after having done nearly everything within their power to imagine, they realize that something is still missing.

There is a space in every person's life that only God can fill. You can have a great career or business, marry the person of your dreams, raise a beautiful family, and still feel inadequate. If you have ever felt that way, you need to know that only God can fill that void. There is no substitute for Him. I encourage you to look to Him because He chose you from the very foundation of the world, and He is the key to filling the emptiness in your life. Once you decide to let Him in, you open the door to receive all He has in store for you. Your life will take on a whole new meaning, and you'll begin to see who you are—God's chosen vessel.

This reminds me of one of my mother's favorite pastimes—making ceramics. I have gone to the ceramic shop with her on several occasions, but I prefer helping with the last step—painting. The complete process of making ceramics is time-consuming, but my mother enjoys every moment of it. When considering what to make, she chooses the mold that will shape her creation and give it the outcome she envisions. She begins with the end in mind.

Likewise, God's plan for each of us involves a process of being molded and shaped into His image. God will touch our hearts, renew our minds, and stretch our faith until we start loving, thinking, and acting like Him. As children of God, we must allow Him to transform us through His Word so that we mirror the image of Jesus.

Walk in His Direction

Before establishing a relationship with God, we are accustomed to doing things our way. But as we walk with Him and learn more about His ways, we begin to realize that certain things cannot remain the same. Regardless of what we think we know, God has a better way and a better plan than anything we can come up with on our own. An example of this is in the Gospel of Matthew:

One day as Jesus was walking along the shore of the Sea of Galilee, he saw two brothers—Simon, also called Peter, and Andrew—throwing a net into the water, for they fished for a living. Jesus called out to them, "Come, follow me, and I will show you how to fish for people!" And they left their nets at once and followed him. A little farther up the shore he saw two other brothers, James and John, sitting in a boat with their father, Zebedee, repairing their nets. And he called them to come, too. They immediately followed him, leaving the boat and their father behind (Matthew 4:18-22, NLT).

In this passage, we can see that Peter, Andrew, James, and John decided to let go of three critical things

6

to their lives and careers. Collectively, they released their nets, boats, and their father's provision for them.

The net in this story is like the types of things we depend on to meet our needs. The problem is that our resources and methods are not always the most reliable. The Bible explains that when Jesus saw James and John, they were mending their nets. That means they were busy trying to fix something that was broken, so they could succeed in what they were trying to accomplish.

Like these disciples, we often spend time trying to mend things on our own before discovering God has the perfect solution. Instead of repairing something that will never work, we should let them go and follow Jesus. The situation needs no further explanation. We already know we have tried to mend the broken nets in our lives, perhaps not just one way, but several ways on many occasions. Yet despite our best efforts, the nets continue to unravel. No one has to tell us our way isn't working. We already know that. The problem is that until He called us, we did not know of any other way. But once we start to understand His guidance better, we must begin to put more trust in His way of doing things.

The boat represents the things we allow to move us. There is nothing wrong with moving when we are going in the right direction. On the other hand, we can move but never reach our intended destination. If you find you are in the same predicament this year that you were in three years ago, look at what you have been allowing to move you. If other people's opinions or past mistakes have driven and misled you, then the solution is simple. Let those things go and follow God. Apply His Word to your life and follow His guidance.

Last, the scriptures tell us James and John left their father. That is significant because parents are responsible for providing for their children while allowing them to mature. Many times, parents and others become too accustomed to helping. They do not realize when it is time to let God intervene. We all need to have personal experience with Jehovah Jireh, the God who provides so that we can see Him as our only real Source. Parents and others block opportunities for people to grow when they dominate situations instead of allowing God to teach His children what He wants them to learn.

Remember: God knows our hearts, and He determines how to carry out His will in our lives. Sometimes we rely too much on other people to do things for us, give something to us, and provide us necessities. It is not God's intent for us to rely too much on other people.

Years ago, when I first started living independently, my income was not enough to meet all my living expenses. One time, I called one of my relatives and asked to borrow money to help with my bills. Surprisingly, she said no. Initially, I became upset and worried because I did not know what I was going to do. The feeling of being without help was frightening and intimidating for a young girl like me. I was also confused. Since I was never the kind of person who looked to others for handouts, I did not understand why my relative wouldn't help me. After all, it was easy to see that I was going through a rough time, even though I was doing what I thought at the time was my best.

After hearing the Word and learning about the need to trust God to provide my needs, I realized that it was not anyone else's responsibility. Philippians 4:19 (KJV) says, "God will supply all of our needs according to his riches in glory by Christ Jesus." So, after that experience, I started applying God's Word to my situations with more intention. One night specifically, I decided to read aloud several scriptures that focused on God's promises for provision. I spoke as though those promises belonged to me, and in fact, they did. Before long, I discovered that I was no longer struggling to make ends meet. I was even able to share what I had with others. When I decided to accept God as my one trustworthy Source, He gave me the wisdom to use what I had in a resourceful manner. Once I learned that valuable lesson, He blessed me with more.

Today, I look for ways to help other people, and I use those same opportunities to tell people about God's goodness. I will never forget the struggle I endured and how God taught me to overcome it by looking, not to other people, but Him. Ever since I learned how to apply God's Word to my situations and trust Him as my provider, my life has never been the same. So, how do you receive what God has for you? The answer is simple. Let go of the tendency to rely on others and follow Him.

You Don't Have to Struggle

I wish I could say that staying connected with God will eliminate all your troubles. Unfortunately, this isn't the case. What I can tell you, though, is that as you walk with God, you'll discover He has the solution to every problem you encounter, including your conflict.

Many people wonder why they still struggle after accepting Christ. It's not that they don't want to do His will. Sometimes we reach a point where we're just not sure what God wants us to do about our situations. During those times, we should aim to minimize distractions and seek God for the answers we need.

Consider the following scripture: "There was a man named Zacchaeus, which was the chief among the publicans, and he was rich. And he sought to see Jesus who he was; and could not for the press, because he was little of stature. And he ran before, and climbed up into a sycamore tree to see him: for he was to pass that way." (Luke 19:2-4, KJV)

Like Zacchaeus, many of us have a hard time seeing Jesus because there is a deluge of distractions in our way. Our thoughts are crowded, our hearts are overwhelmed, and too much is happening at once. We tend to focus on things in our immediate view, but like Zaccaeus, we need to go up a little higher. Over the years, I have learned that the way up is down. That means to excel, we must first humble ourselves. As a starting point, we need to get down on our knees and pray! To see beyond the surface of things, we have to establish a prayer life, develop a lifestyle that puts God first, and trust Him to show us what we need to do. When we do this, we'll begin seeing Him in a way we have never seen Him before.

Sometimes our choices create conflict. God's love allows us the freedom to decide what we want to do, but He also provides us with truthful answers to help us make the right decisions. When our choices don't coincide with His Word, we struggle. When we finally decide to give up the fight and accept God's way, we have more inner peace along with the confidence in knowing that in time, the struggles will subside.

Understand, too, that struggles and opposition often come from being involved with things that are just plain wrong. 1 Peter 5:8 (KJV) says, "Be sober, be vigilant, because your adversary the devil, as a roaring lion, walketh about, seeking whom he may devour."

The enemy looks for ways to devour God's people, so pay close attention to what happens in your life and ensure you are not assisting the enemy in his many attempts to defeat you. If you sin against God, you're giving the enemy permission to torment you without even realizing it. We are going to make mistakes without question. But we need to shut every door to the intentional practice of doing things we know are wrong. In John 14:30-31 (AMP), Jesus said, "… the prince, evil genius, ruler of the world is coming. And he has no claim on Me. He has nothing in common with Me, there is nothing in Me that belongs to him, and he has no power over Me." If you are harboring things like resentment, hatred, and envy, make up your mind to let them go with God's help. If you stand firm on God's promises and resist the enemy's temptations, he will find nothing in you that belongs to him.

Furthermore, if he tries to come against you, he will be trespassing. James 4:7 (KJV) says, "Submit yourselves therefore to God. Resist the devil, and he will flee from you."

Today I encourage you to receive what God has in store for you by welcoming His will. Know His way is perfect, and He always knows what is best for you. Trust Him to direct you. Let go of conflict and search for the truth in His Word.

CHAPTER 1 SUMMARY

How can accepting God's plan for you make a difference in your life?

Describe a time when you had to let go of something that was not right for you. How did this experience impact you?

Identify your net, boat, and areas where you have been relying too much on someone or something else.

Based on your personal experiences, explain the importance of relying more on God than on other people?

Thoughts for Reflection

CHAPTER 2

Have Confidence in God

Trust in the LORD with all thine heart, and lean not unto thine own understanding. In all thy ways acknowledge him, and he shall direct thy paths.

–Proverbs 3:5-6, KJV

After the stock market plummeted some years ago, I listened to an upset woman speak about how much money she lost in her investments. She expressed how disappointed she was after years of investing her hard-earned money. "I am finished with the stock market," she said, "I will never do that again." After enduring such a painful experience combined with the uncertainty of our nation's economy, this woman's confidence in the stock market was a thing of the past. Even after the economy started to recover and the value of stocks increased, the painful reminder of what happened was probably enough to discourage her from taking another risk.

Most of us can relate to this example. At some point in all of our lives, we have relied on something that eventually failed. Maybe it was a particular type of vehicle worth less than what we paid for it, a relationship that ended, or a business deal that didn't work out. Depending on the situation, you might have decided not to take another chance on something that disappointed you once before.

No one likes the feeling of being let down. No one wants to have their dreams crushed right before their eyes. While taking risks is inevitable, we still have to consider what might happen if things do not pan out the way we expect.

Confidence, according to Webster's dictionary, is "the quality or state of being certain." When you are sure of something, there is no room for any doubt. As believers, we can be sure God will do everything he has promised, despite our previous disappointments. Leave no room for doubt. Instead, trust and know for sure that God is with you every step of the way, no matter what you face. In the scriptures, Luke 18 discusses several vital principles that pertain to maintaining complete confidence in God.

Principle #1:

Never Give Up

One day Jesus told his disciples a story to emphasize the importance of praying without giving up. There was a judge in a certain city," he said, "who neither feared God nor cared about people. A widow of that city came to him repeatedly, saying, 'Give me justice in this dispute with my enemy.' The judge ignored her for a while, but finally, he said to himself, 'I don't fear God or care about people, but this woman is driving me crazy. I'm going to see that she gets justice because she is wearing me out with her constant requests! Then Jesus said, "Learn a lesson from this unjust judge. Even he rendered a just decision in the end. So don't you think God will surely give justice to his chosen people who cry out to him day and night? Will he keep putting them off? I tell you, he will grant justice to them quickly! But when the Son of Man returns, how many will he find on the earth who have faith?" (Luke 18:1-8, NLT).

The first thing Jesus mentions in this passage is that we should always pray and not lose heart. He emphasizes this point because He knows the enemy will try to hinder us from seeing the fulfillment of God's promises. Since the enemy can't stop God from blessing us, he will try to prevent us from believing. Hebrews 11:6 tells us that without faith, it is impossible to please God. It is difficult, if not impossible, to receive anything if you don't believe you'll have it. That is why Jesus' statement about perseverance in prayer is so vital. When we pray, our trust in the Lord becomes the bridge that connects our request to the answer we receive. In this parable, Jesus said He would avenge us quickly. But when He shows up for us, what will our frame of mind be? Are we going to lose hope before seeing the answers to our prayers, or will we keep the faith? We must trust God consistently and stand firm, knowing He will honor His promises.

Principle #2:

Trust Only in God's Righteousness

Then Jesus told this story to some who had great confidence in their righteousness and scorned everyone else: "Two men went to the Temple to pray. One was a Pharisee, and the other was a despised tax collector. The Pharisee stood by himself and prayed this prayer: 'I thank you, God, that I am not a sinner like everyone else. For I don't cheat, I don't sin, and I don't commit adultery. I'm certainly not like that tax collector! I fast twice a week, and I give you a tenth of my income.' "But the tax collector stood at a distance and dared not even lift his eyes to heaven as he prayed. Instead, he beat his chest in sorrow, saying, 'O God, be merciful to me, for I am a sinner.' I tell you, this sinner, not the Pharisee, returned home justified before God. For those who exalt themselves will be humbled, and those who humble themselves will be exalted (Luke 18:9-14, NLT).

God's gifts are not merit-based; they are love-based. Those who are willing to humble themselves and recognize the need for God's continuous grace are the ones He esteems the highest. He is not impressed with the ones who boast about their good deeds while putting other people down. If we genuinely desire to walk in the fullness of God's power, we cannot take the credit for what He does. Neither should we attempt to trust in our righteousness. Without Him, we have no righteousness at all. As you walk with Christ, your complete confidence must be in Him.

Principle #3:

Trust in God's Resources

Once a religious leader asked Jesus this question: "Good Teacher, what should I do to inherit eternal life?" "Why do you call me good?" Jesus asked him. "Only God is truly good. But to answer your question, you know the commandments: 'You must not commit adultery. You must not murder. You must not steal. You must not testify falsely. Honor your father and mother.' The man replied, "I've obeyed all these commandments since I was young." When Jesus heard his answer, he said, "There is still one thing you haven't done. Sell all your possessions and give the money to the poor, and you will have treasure in heaven. Then come, follow me." But when the man heard this, he became very sad, for he was very rich. When Jesus saw this, he said, "How hard it is for the rich to enter the Kingdom of God! In fact, it is easier for a camel to go through the eye of a needle than for a rich person to enter the Kingdom of God!" Those who heard this said, "Then who in the world can be saved?" He replied, "What is impossible for people is possible with God." Peter said, "We've left our homes to follow you." "Yes," Jesus replied, "and I assure you that everyone who has given up house or wife or brothers or parents or children, for the sake of the Kingdom of God, will be repaid many times over in this life, and will have eternal life in the world to come. (Luke 18:18-30, NLT)

This passage reveals that we shouldn't attempt to rely on our resources more than we rely on God. An exceedingly wealthy ruler approached Jesus and wanted to know how to inherit eternal life. When Jesus told the ruler to give up everything he had and become His disciple, he walked away disappointed.

The wealthy ruler was unaware of two critical points. First, those who give up everything to follow Jesus will receive much more in return. Second, believers receive the promise of eternal life. So, it did not matter how wealthy this leader was. If he had more confidence in God than in His resources, he would have received far more than he could have imagined – on earth and in heaven! We must be willing to give up everything we think we have to accept all God that has for us.

Principle #4:

Be Persistent in Prayer!

As Jesus approached Jericho, a blind beggar was sitting beside the road. When he heard the noise of a crowd going past, he asked what was happening. They told him that Jesus the Nazarene was going by. So, he began shouting, "Jesus, Son of David, have mercy on me!" "Be quiet!" the people in front yelled at him. But he only shouted louder, "Son of David, have mercy on me!" When Jesus heard him, he stopped and ordered that the man is brought to him. As the man came near, Jesus asked him, "What do you want me to do for you?"

"Lord," he said, "I want to see!" And Jesus said, "All right, receive your sight! Your faith has healed you." Instantly the man could see, and he followed Jesus, praising God. And all who saw it praised God, too (Luke 18:35-43, NLT).

When we pursue God, we should never allow others to stop us, no matter what they say. In this passage, we find a blind man crying out to God for mercy. As he shouted, the other people in the crowd tried to quiet him. Instead of stopping, the blind man cried out even more! That is when Jesus heard him. Because of the blind man's persistence, a miracle took place in his life.

Some believe that what stopped Jesus in His tracks was the intensity of the man's cry. It is also safe to say that this man's willingness to continue pursuing Jesus, despite the crowd's opposition, moved Him to respond. It was the blind man's faith that captured Jesus' attention. When you demonstrate bold confidence that says, "I refuse to allow anyone to stop me from believing in God's promises," He will make sure you receive what you need.

Confidence in the Face of Difficulty

While serving in the military, I completed several confidence courses that consisted of low crawling through tunnels and under barbed wire, climbing ropes and walls, and many other challenging obstacles. These courses are designed to have no choice but to use strength, endurance, and speed to make it through. Most of us did not recognize we possessed these qualities. Sometimes, we had to work as a team and help each other succeed. By the end, we were all exhausted but felt a tremendous sense of accomplishment. Just knowing we made it through successfully reassured us to stay strong for future challenges. We felt that because we made it through those difficult challenges, we could accomplish just about anything.

Similarly, we face many obstacles while going through life's confidence courses. As we deal with each encounter, we will find ourselves using God's strength to make it through. Sometimes, He will send others to help us. As Christians, we have to remember we're all on the same team. When one of us makes it through a challenge, we all make it through because we are one.

For example, in 1994, I lost my grandmother to heart disease. I didn't know how I could bounce back from the pain I felt when she died. She was my best friend. In fact, after losing her, I was never the same. I felt alone in the world, without anyone to trust. I also thought no one could love me as my grandmother did. What on earth was I going to do?

I remember leaving while the funeral was still in progress to go into the church's prayer room and cry out some of the pain I was feeling. One of my mother's closest friends came to me, hugged me, and began to tell me how my grandmother was in a better place because she was no longer suffering. As I continued to cry, I thought to myself, "But I love her..." Then, to my amazement, my mother's friend said aloud, "Yes, yes, but He loves her too..." It shocked me because nothing like that had ever happened to me before! How did she know what I was thinking, let alone feeling in my heart? I knew right then that God sent my mother's friend to let me know He loved both of us, and He would take care of me. Although my grandmother and I are now apart, we are both experiencing the love of Christ. The love I thought I would never receive again came to me through Him above and beyond what my grandmother or anyone could have ever given me. He became my best friend.

As I think now about the confidence courses, I imagine when I felt I had no strength to love again. God strengthened me so that I could continue to make it through every confidence course life presents. He still does it to this very day. And, He will do the same for you.

Have Confidence in God's Ability

Our trust in God helps us recognize He has given us the authority to do what we cannot imagine ourselves being able to do without Him. Because of God's power, we can declare the promises of God's Word over our lives. We do not have to wonder if God hears us when we pray. Instead, when we ask God for something according to His will, we already know He will bring it to pass. We must also remember to acknowledge that it is God who equips us with our abilities. He empowers us to accomplish things in life; we cannot do anything alone.

Years ago, I attended a leadership development course that consisted of land navigation training and testing. During the training, we refreshed our skills in map reading, pace counting, and land navigation. We practiced each of the steps involved several times before taking the test. I was confident that I knew what to do, and I was right. When test day arrived, we were on our own. To pass the course, we had to locate three of the four assigned points. We plotted our points on our maps and were dropped off at our starting location. I located my first and second points with no problems.

When the time came to find my third point, however, I somehow became lost. Upset, I began to panic. The test was timed, and if I didn't complete the test within the allotted time, I would be considered a "no go." In other words, I would have failed.

While lost in the middle of nowhere, I began to talk to God. One of the things I said was, "I know that You wouldn't bring me to this point and then allow me to fail. This just isn't the way You do things, God." Then I stopped worrying and began to praise God. My attitude shifted from fear and panic to complete confidence in God. Somehow, I knew I was going to pass that land navigation course. Failure was not an option.

About ten minutes after that conversation, I looked up and realized I was at my third point. I have no idea how it happened, and I didn't have time to figure it out! I quickly annotated the point on my answer sheet. Realizing I was close to the finishing point, I ran back and turned in my answers. I passed the land navigation test with only 90 seconds to spare.

That experience taught me that no matter how confident I am in my abilities, my confidence in God truly makes the difference.

Thoughts for Reflection

CHAPTER 3

See the Lord as Your Shepherd

Psalm 23 is one of my favorite passages of scripture. It reminds me that no one can look out for us the way God can. He created and knows everything about us. He also knows exactly what we need and when. His unconditional love reassures us He has our best interests at heart. If we only look to Him, we will discover that He is willing and able to keep us securely in His care.

The LORD is my shepherd; I shall not want. He maketh me to lie down in green pastures: he leadeth me beside the still waters. He restoreth my soul: he leadeth me in the paths of righteousness for his name's sake. Yea, though I walk through the valley of the shadow of death, I will fear no evil: for thou art with me; thy rod and thy staff they comfort me. Thou preparest a table before me in the presence of mine enemies: thou anointest my head with oil; my cup runneth over. Surely goodness and mercy shall follow me all the days of my life: and I will dwell in the house of the Lord forever. (Psalm 23, KJV).

There is an old story about two men who quoted this 23rd Psalm at a public event. The first man was young, vibrant, and well educated. He was an eloquent speaker. When it was his turn to speak, he rose and quoted Psalm 23 with grace and precision. When he concluded reciting it, the audience gave him a standing ovation. The second speaker was an elderly man who appeared rugged and worn from life. Age had progressively slowed his movements. As he slowly made his way to the podium, he also began to recite the passage from Psalm 23. When this elderly man recited the passage, however, he did so with depth, passion, and intensity. By the time he had finished, nearly the entire audience was moved to tears. A young boy from the audience leaned over to his mother and said, "I don't get it. They both said the same thing. Why was everyone so moved by the second speech?" The mother replied, "Son, it's quite obvious. While the first speaker clearly knew the Psalm, there's no doubt whatsoever that the elderly man knows the Shepherd."

Do you know the Lord as your Shepherd? Do you recognize His hand of protection over your life? Let's pause for a moment and think about these questions. God wants to be involved in your life situations. He desires to be the one who ensures all your needs are met. Our role is to recognize Him as the one to whom we owe full credit for providing us with direction, provision, rest, peace and tranquility, courage, protection, and restoration.

Allow God to Direct Your Paths

There used to be a time when traveling unfamiliar paths led to wrong turns, lost time, and frustration. Today, thanks to satellite technology, we have Global Positioning Systems (GPS), making it easier to reach our planned destination, while minimizing the risk of getting lost. If you make a wrong turn, the navigation system will suggest rerouting options to get you back on course, so you can arrive at your destination with few difficulties.

When the Lord directs us, the paths on which He leads are always the most appropriate for our lives, even when we don't realize it. Sometimes we get off course by choice or due to distractions along the way. But Jesus redirects us and ensures we resume the course we're supposed to take. When you have to make an important decision and need direction, take time to acknowledge your Shepherd, and remind yourself, "He leads me in the paths of righteousness for His name's sake" (Psalm 23:3, KJV). Then ask yourself, "Is my chosen path morally right? Does it honor God? Is my movement syncopated with God's timing?" If your answers are yes, continue moving forward. If not, allow Him to redirect you according to His plan for you.

Trust Him for Provision

Every time I see an award show on television, I look forward to hearing what the recipient has to say. I look to see if, at any point in the speech, they'll take time to recognize God for getting them to the level of success they reached. When they acknowledge Him, I get excited, because it shows they understand whose power is really at work. We have many gifts, talents, and abilities, but we didn't get them by coincidence. The Lord provided us with everything we need to be successful.

Rest in Him

I have witnessed friends working on multiple tasks, rarely allowing time for a break. Even while at the point of burnout, they continue pressing and working and doing what they believe needs to be done at that time. If they push themselves too hard, unfortunately, their immune system may begin to weaken and they are forced to take a break due to a cold or similar illness. Then they say things such as, "Well, I wasn't listening to my body, and I ended up getting sick."

God never expects us to overwork ourselves for the sake of accomplishment. While hard work is rewarding, it should never be something that wears us out to the point of complete exhaustion. One of the requirements from God is that you rest frequently. It shows you trust Him enough to get things done through His strength and power, not yours.

Studies have shown that inadequate rest has a negative impact on our cognitive ability. It also interferes with our body's natural healing process. To remain highly effective, we must look out for our physical well-being. Getting the proper rest ensures that we are able to function properly. I admit there are times when I take on too many tasks at one time. So many of us, including me, have had to learn to say "no" when necessary. Otherwise, we'll find ourselves going through periods of irritability and moodiness—additional signs that indicate the need for rest. If we do not take the time to relax, our efforts become ineffective, and we pose the risk of doing more harm than good, both to others and ourselves. I encourage you, therefore, to take time out for rejuvenation. Doing so will replenish your body, mind, and spirit. It will also add years to your life. You will discover that you are able to work more efficiently and produce greater results.

Trust His Will

One of the many things I love about God is He loves us for who we are. That is why it is okay for us to be honest with Him. After all, He knows everything anyway! While we don't want to enter a cycle of complaining, the Lord welcomes our openness. But somewhere in the midst of all, we are saying, there has to be a "nevertheless" that comes from our heart –

"…nevertheless, not my will but thine be done" (Luke 22:42, KJV).

I learned this very important principle when talking with my dad about a difficult situation I encountered. After receiving my first graduate degree, I transitioned from the military and entered the civilian workforce with high hopes of having a solid career. I accepted a position for what felt like my dream job and was very excited about it. Life was great! That is until my husband received military orders and we had to relocate. Well, I had a choice to make – I could have either remained at the current location to keep my promising new career steady, or relocate and keep the family stable. After my family and I prayed and talked everything over, we decided it was best to relocate together.

When I made this decision, I was confident that God was so pleased, He would quickly reward me for selflessly letting my career go for the sake of my family's stability. Unfortunately, it didn't quite happen the way I expected. While searching diligently to find a new job, I prayed, read the Word, and did all I knew to do. Yet for a long time, nothing happened. In fact, I watched other people with less work experience obtain positions quickly, while I remained unemployed.

When I talked to my dad, I expected him to say something like, "I agree you really should be moving forward in your career at this stage in your life. God will give you the desires of your heart. It won't be much longer; just hold on and you'll see." Instead, his advice went something like this: "If you truly want to honor God, you have to learn to accept His will, regardless of what it looks like to you." Then he went on to tell me about what Jesus went through in the garden of Gethsemane (See Matthew 26). Well, I knew my dad was telling me the truth, but I just didn't want to hear it – not then. I had my heart set on getting my career back on track. So, for a while, I stopped calling my dad. I just didn't want to hear anything about the garden of Gethsemane.

My first response to my career situation, or lack thereof, was to ask questions. "What is going on? Have I done something wrong? Should I have prayed about this a little longer before I chose to leave my job? Did I make the right decision?" If you have ever been in a similar situation, I'm sure you had moments where you wondered what was really going on. With this context, I can clear up a common misconception. I have heard people say, "Don't question God." The truth is God does not mind us asking Him questions. He does mind, though, when we second-guess Him. God expects us to ask questions about our lives. After all, He is the only one with the answers! Proverbs 4:7 (KJV) says, "Wisdom is the principal thing; therefore, get wisdom: and with all thy getting get understanding," so how can we obtain understanding if we don't ask questions? God wants us to go to Him and ask whenever we are not sure about something, no matter what it is.

It is also important to understand when we make decisions, we need to take full responsibility for them. Don't blame anyone for the decisions you make if the outcome is not what you expected. Have the willingness to accept your choices. In my situation, no matter which path I chose, there would have been problems; there was no way around it. The question then became, "Which consequences would I rather deal with for an indefinite period of time?" Regardless of how I felt about the situation, there was no way to avoid having my own personal "not my will" experience. It is where I came to know the Shepherd in an up-close and personal way.

During this season of my life, I prayed and read the Bible more often. The more time I spent with Him, the more at home I felt being in His presence. This time also helped me gain a better understanding of His intentions for my well-being. At first, I looked for tangible differences. Then I realized that while God is more than able to provide us with tangible blessings, it was time for me to discover real treasures. He was doing with me what no amount of money could buy! As our Shepherd, the Lord knows exactly what we need. In fact, He knows better than we could ever begin to know. Remember, He works things out in our hearts so that we fit His custom-designed plan for our lives.

After nearly a year of experiencing unemployment and eating humble pie, I reentered the workforce a changed person. As a wife and a mom, I was more patient, loving, and supportive than before, but all the time before, I didn't realize these were areas in my life that needed work.

As our Shepherd, we can rest assured He will take very good care of us. When we go through challenging and uncomfortable situations, He promises to continue being right there with us. We can rest knowing God will guide us, protect us, and meet our needs, as long as we look to Him.

Thank Him

Being faced with challenges in life is inevitable, but you are empowered to overcome each of them. God equipped you with the ability to rule over your storms. I must admit many times it certainly does not seem that I have this ability. I remember one evening while praying, I said to God, "I'm in a position that makes me feel as though I have nothing to contribute to others. How can I encourage others to reach for the best when I am not seeing results in my own life?" The Holy Spirit answered my question with this revelation: Jesus was in the boat with His disciples as they were going through a terrible storm. He wasn't someplace far off, giving advice from a distance. Rather, He encouraged the disciples while He was going through that storm with them! Then He demonstrated how to overcome it.

Jesus himself showed us that to be effective in helping others, it is necessary to go through challenges and demonstrate how to overcome them using what God has taught us. How do you really know that what you tell others will actually work, unless you have experienced it for yourself?

Having a relationship with God does not exempt us from experiencing times of trouble. But the good news is when we have a relationship with God, He gives us the courage to face our problems, the wisdom to know how to handle them, patience to endure them, and finally, the power to overcome.

Romans 8:37 says we are more than conquerors. This means we don't just win; we win big. Therefore, we shouldn't make it a habit to avoid every challenge we encounter. Instead, fight to win, and use the situation as an opportunity to add wisdom to your life. There is a lesson for us in every situation we encounter. God will not lead us up to a certain point and then just abandon us. Sometimes we need to pause and consider what we are learning along the way.

Also, keep in mind, not every challenge comes from the enemy. Sometimes God will allow us to experience circumstances to develop our character and remind us of the importance of gratitude. He doesn't want us to overlook the small things in life and begin to think He is obligated to give us whatever we desire. Instead, He wants us to have a genuine appreciation for who He is at all times, whether things seem to be going our way or not. God wants us to love Him simply because He loves us. "I will bless the Lord at all times: His praise shall continuously be in my mouth," (Psalm 34:1, KJV).

CHAPTER 3 SUMMARY

In what specific areas of your life do you need to see the Lord as your Shepherd?

What steps do you plan to take to place those areas in His care?

How can we use our storms as opportunities to encourage others?

What outcome should we expect when choosing to walking with God through challenging times, rather than attempting to avoid them?

Thoughts for Reflection

CHAPTER 4

Love

God's love is so powerful that despite His infinite wisdom, He has given us the freedom to make our own choices, even knowing we will often make the wrong ones. Take the time to reflect on the worst thing you have ever done. Now realize that God already knew what was going to happen before it occurred. Yet His love for you remained. He knew how many times you would apologize for the same mistakes. He also knew that you would often make promises and break them.

Nevertheless, your shortcomings have never caused God to love you any less. You can do nothing to change His love for you or earn His love through your own effort. He has provided all His children with an abundance of mercy and unmerited favor. We are endowed with the gift of love when we receive Jesus Christ into our lives and accept Him as our personal Lord and Savior.

Love Yourself

I want to thank one of my dearest relatives for imparting this important principle in my life. During a conversation, I shared some things that were bothering me. My relative listened for a while and then responded with two simple questions. His first question was, "What is the greatest commandment in the Bible?" I said, "Love the Lord with all of your heart." Then, he asked, "What is the second commandment?" I responded, "Love your neighbor as yourself." Finally, he stated, "Repeat that last part." I said, "As yourself." Then he said, "Until you learn to love yourself, you cannot love anyone else."

That 30-minute conversation changed my perspective in a major way. Suddenly I realized that when you develop a genuine love for God, the first person He teaches you to love is yourself. You must care for yourself enough to want exactly what God wants for you—the very best that life has to offer. Furthermore, you have to care for your own well-being before you can truly help anyone else.

Love Others

When we have developed a love for God and for ourselves, we are then able to love our neighbor as God commands. I always like to say that love is an action word. It involves doing what is good toward others, without hesitating and without selfish motives. We should have a genuine concern for our neighbors' well-being. This is the greatest of all commands.

Love is the most powerful force that exists in our world today. When we love one another, we bring out the best in one another. Imagine the possibilities that would exist if multitudes of people had each other's best interest at heart and were completely free from selfish motives. Although it is almost impossible for most people to imagine, with God all things are possible. He would never command us to do something we could not accomplish. Genuine love represents who God is. When we allow love to show, God gets the glory every time.

"If I could speak all the languages of earth and of angels, but didn't love others, I would only be a noisy gong or a clanging cymbal. If I had the gift of prophecy, and if I understood all of God's secret plans and possessed all knowledge, and if I had such faith that I could move mountains, but didn't love others, I would be nothing. If I gave everything I have to the poor and even sacrificed my body, I could boast about it but if I didn't love others, I would have gained nothing. Love is patient and kind. Love is not jealous or boastful or proud or rude. It does not demand its own way. It is not irritable, and it keeps no record of being wronged. It does not rejoice about injustice but rejoices whenever the truth wins out. Love never gives up, never loses faith, is always hopeful, and endures through every circumstance. Prophecy and speaking in unknown language and special knowledge will become useless. But love will last forever!" (1 Corinthians 13:1-8, NLT)

Giving – an Expression of Love

Giving is a form of demonstrating love and is a significant part of every believer's life. God gives to us, and in turn, He expects us to do the same for others. The best example of giving according to God's heart can be found in John 3:16. It says, "For God so loved the world, that he gave his only begotten Son, that whosoever believeth in him should not perish, but have everlasting life" (KJV). There are a number of ways to demonstrate love through giving. Whether it is time spent listening to a friend and sharing advice or giving donations to your favorite charity, you should know that your gift matters. Giving of ourselves, our talents, and our resources help extend God's love.

Offer Gifts to Those in Need

Another way to demonstrate God's love is by helping to meet the needs of His people. When we give according to God's heart, we create an opportunity for God to demonstrate His love through us. An example of this is found in the gospel of Matthew when Jesus fed 5,000 people who had followed him and listened to His teachings until the evening fell upon them. The disciples were about to send the people away to buy their own food. Instead, Matthew 14:16-21 (AMP) explains,

Jesus said, they do not need to go away; you give them something to eat. They said to Him, We have nothing here but five loaves and two fish. He said, Bring them here to Me. Then He ordered the crowds to recline on the grass; and He took the five loaves and the two fish, and, looking up to heaven, He gave thanks and blessed and broke the loaves and handed the pieces to the disciples, and the disciples gave them to the people. And they all ate and were satisfied. And they picked up twelve baskets full of the broken pieces left over. And those who ate were about 5,000 men, not including women and children.

Instead of sending the people away, Jesus met their needs by feeding them right there in the wilderness. In doing so, He demonstrated the kind of love and compassion He expects us to demonstrate toward each other. In fact, the way we treat other people is a direct reflection of our love for God. Helping to meet the needs of God's people is one of the ways we express our love for God.

In the gospel of John, we find that Jesus had a conversation with Peter in which He asked Peter several times if he loved Him: "A third time he asked him, "Simon son of John, do you love me?" Peter was hurt that Jesus asked the question a third time. He said, "Lord, you know everything. You know that I love you." Jesus said, "Then feed my sheep.," (John 21:17, NLT).

The Lord desires that we demonstrate our love through the way we treat others. Remember to see love as an action word. Love God, yourself, and others. Your demonstration of God's love may lead others to want to know Him for themselves.

CHAPTER 4 SUMMARY

Give an example of a time you saw evidence of God's lovingkindness?

Why is it so important to share this same experience with others?

What is the correct response when dealing with offensive situations?

How does pride damage one's relationship with God?

Thoughts for Reflection

CHAPTER 5

Study God's Word

I came across an interesting quote one day: "Many people will lie, cheat, and steal to get ahead when all they have to do is read." It is one of the main pathways that can lead to success in many areas. Reading and studying God's word is instrumental in helping us discover who we are and who God created us to become.

In the book of Jeremiah, God spoke the following words: "Before I formed you in the womb I knew and approved of you as My chosen instrument, and before you were born I separated and set you apart, consecrating you; and I appointed you as a prophet to the nations" (Jeremiah 1:5, AMP).

In this scripture, God revealed His purpose and plan for Jeremiah's life. No longer did Jeremiah have to wonder about why he existed. God made it clear that he was a chosen prophet. From that moment, no matter what anyone else said about Jeremiah, he knew the truth. Nothing else mattered except what God had already told him about who he was.

The answer to any questions you might have about who you are and your purpose in life can be found only in the Creator. Studying the Word of God reveals the truth about your existence and the plans God has for you. Dismiss anything negative that people have spoken about you, and believe God created you for a great and wonderful purpose. He has equipped you with the ability to do the impossible and the unimaginable.

Pause and Reflect

Meditating on God's Word is a significant part of maintaining our relationship with Him. When we meditate on the Word, we go beyond reading the scriptures and begin a process of reflective thinking. By doing so, we consider how the Word applies to our situations—past, present, and future. Because God desires that we live successful lives, He provided solutions to all of our problems in His Word. It is up to us to read, meditate, calmly reflect on, and observe the scriptures. When we do, we will gain more wisdom and insight, making the Word relevant and beneficial to our lives.

In Joshua 1:8 (KJV), God gave the following instructions to Joshua: "This book of the law shall not depart out of thy mouth; but thou shalt meditate therein day and night, that thou mayest observe to do according to all that is written therein: For then thou shalt make thy way prosperous, and then thou shalt have good success."

Meditating on God's Word also allows us to gain spiritual insight into what He has to say concerning us. It is possible to read the same scripture several times and understand it from various perspectives each time. The Word is one avenue that God will use to speak to you personally about your circumstances.

For example, one afternoon, while studying Mark Chapter 6, I received an insight that I had never received before from that particular passage of scripture. It describes the miracle Jesus performed when he fed 5,000 people, beginning only with two fish and five loaves of bread. What I had not noticed until I studied the chapter that afternoon was that when Jesus provided instructions for all of the people to sit down in the green grass (see Mark 6:39), He was preparing them to receive something from heaven. But the first thing they needed to do was get in the right position to receive what they needed. They had to organize themselves, sit down, and relax. Once this happened, Jesus took what was available, looked up to heaven, blessed it, and distributed it (see Mark 6:41).

At that moment, I realized that whenever we need to accomplish something that seems impossible, we must (1) posture ourselves to receive what we need, (2) see past our limited ability, (3) look toward heaven, (4) bless; that is, speak well of and thank God for what we currently have, and (5) start using what we have at that moment. In turn, God will add His supernatural ability to help us achieve what might seem impossible.

Some common phrases express this principle: bloom where you're planted; don't despise small beginnings; use what you've got. God will meet and exceed our expectations—but we have to do our part. God is no respecter of person. Just as He gave me insight into how to apply His Word to my life situations, He will do the same for you as you take the time to study His Word consistently.

Competence begets Confidence

When someone comes to you for help, they want to be sure that you know what you're doing. For example, when you begin a new job, you are expected to learn every aspect of your job. As your level of proficiency grows, your confidence increases. When you are serious enough about the job, you work diligently to learn everything required of you. If you continue in this manner, you'll eventually become known as a subject matter expert.

This principle also applies to proficiency in learning God's Word. Diligently studying God's Word causes you to become "… a worker who does not need to be ashamed, rightly dividing the word of truth" (See 2 Timothy 2:15, NKJV). When you have developed substantial knowledge and skill in applying God's Word, you'll become more effective at improving your life and helping others.

Being skillful in God's Word involves reading and studying the Bible. However, it doesn't necessarily stop there because the application is what makes the information relevant. Knowledge is a precursor to experience, and we need both to be effective. Take music, for instance. An interest in music might motivate you to want to learn more about it. You could decide to study the history of music and different instruments. But knowing about music doesn't make you a musician. Once you develop music skills such as singing or playing an instrument, you can begin sharing your talent with other people. Similarly, when we are skillful in applying God's Word, it means we know how to use it effectively when dealing with life's circumstances.

Putting God's Word into practice leads to changes in many areas of our lives. If you feel as though you are waiting for God to do something, consider this possibility – you might already have the solution. It could very well be up to you to find the answer by studying God's Word. Read, study, meditate, and practice applying the scriptures to your life consistently. As you allow God to change you through His Word, you will also begin to see your situations change. The more you practice using God's Word, the more your life will improve.

The Value of Consistency

Anything we do consistently will provide some type of results in our lives. This principle applies to both good and bad habits. For example, if you eat junk food regularly, it will eventually become a habit that can result in poor health. On the other hand, if you establish an exercise routine and practice it regularly, your health may improve. Similarly, if you consistently invest time with God in prayer, meditation, and study, your spiritual development will improve. But if you neglect to invest time with God, you will not experience significant spiritual growth.

To keep the influences of everyday life situations at bay, our time with God needs to be a consistent priority for us. We never want to make the mistake of placing more value on our circumstances than we do on what God has promised us in His Word. Instead, we need to safeguard our faith so that it increases and manifests good results.

In Matthew 17:20, Jesus said, "If you have faith as a mustard seed, you will say to this mountain, 'Move from here to there,' and it will move, and nothing will be impossible for you."

A mustard seed starts very small, but nurturing gives it the potential to mature into a plant with many beneficial qualities. Likewise, when we develop consistency in building our relationship with God, our faith will grow and increase to such magnitude that we can accomplish the seemingly impossible.

God's Powerful Authority

Not only does God's Word help us change our own lives, but it also has the power to impact the things around us. Hebrews 4:12 (AMP) says, "For the word of God that speaks is alive and full of power, making it active, operative, energizing and effective; it is sharper than any two-edged sword, penetrating to the dividing line of the breath of life (soul) and the immortal spirit, and of joints and marrow of the deepest parts of our nature, exposing and sifting and analyzing and judging the very thoughts and purposes of the heart."

A while back, I noticed that whenever I took the time to read God's Word before starting work each day, my atmosphere remained peaceful. Co-workers cooperated and worked well together. We met our deadlines and resolved challenges with few problems.

On the days that I did not read or declare God's Word in my environment, though, there appeared to be much chaos and confusion. Was this a coincidence? I seriously doubt it. God's Word is quick and powerful enough to produce effects that will guarantee victory in our situations. To succeed in our lives, we must develop a lifestyle of consistently putting God's Word into action.

The Bread of Life

Another thing to note about God's Word is that it provides us with spiritual nourishment, which sustains our growth and strength. Many people wonder why things begin to go wrong in their lives when they slack off from praying and studying the Bible. It is not that they have forgotten what the scriptures say. Rather, they have disconnected themselves from the power source - the Word of God. Malnourishment leads to vulnerability. Just as our physical bodies weaken and become susceptible to germs and viruses when we do not eat properly, we become spiritually weak when we do not partake of and digest God's Word.

From a physical perspective, growth and development occur when we consume a variety of nutrients. Consider babies, for instance. When babies are born, their only nourishment comes from milk. It is not until they begin to grow and develop that they progress to solid foods. It would make no sense for a developing child and has all of his or her teeth to receive milk only. That child would become malnourished.

When it comes to our spirituality, we progress from learning the basic principles of God's Word to gaining in-depth knowledge and understanding. For the children of God to grow to their full capacity and prosper, we need to make the Word of God a full-course meal.

Hebrews 5:12-14 (AMP) says, "You have come to need milk, not solid food. For everyone who continues to feed on milk is obviously inexperienced and unskilled in the doctrine of righteousness, for he is a mere infant, not able to talk yet! But solid food is for full-grown men, for those whose senses and mental faculties are trained by practice to discriminate and distinguish between what is morally good and noble and what is evil and contrary either to divine or human law."

As we develop our skill in God's Word, we will accurately distinguish the difference between what is right and wrong without looking for the grey areas as many of us tend to do. There will be no more second-guessing or compromising the truth when we have developed the maturity level described in Hebrews 5. As we continue to mature through studying the Bible, we will achieve real prosperity—the ability to reinvest the spiritual deposits that God makes into our lives by sharing them with others.

Chapter 5 Summary

What benefits are associated with studying God's Word?

How important is it to develop consistent study habits?

What can happen if we slack off from studying?

Why is Jesus referred to as the "Bread of Life?"

Thoughts for Reflection

CHAPTER 6

Manage Your Thoughts

When everything around you is quiet, and you can hear God speaking to your heart, what is He saying to you? What plan is He revealing to you about your life? To answer those questions, you must be able to stay focused on the thoughts God places in your heart. If the situations around you are not adding value to your life, then they are distractions. Distractions come in many forms, and it is often difficult to initially see them for what they are.

When you invest time in God's presence, He will give you insight, helping you become more aware of things to avoid. Remember that when you trust and acknowledge Him, He will direct your paths (see Proverbs 3:5-6).

As you are going through the challenge of eliminating distractions around you, the Holy Spirit's voice can often seem faint. Being in a place where you cannot hear God is not a good thing. You have to do your part to shut off the louder sounds so that you can listen to Him. Make quiet time for Him daily. Remember that time with God should always be your priority.

The book of Joshua provides key verses that expound on the importance of studying and meditating on God's Word. Joshua 1:8 (KJV) says, "This Book of the Law shall not depart out of your mouth, but you shall meditate on it day and night, that you may observe and do according to all that is written in it. For then you shall make your way prosperous, and then you shall deal wisely and have good success."

When Joshua assumed his leadership role over the tribe of Israel, God told him he could make his way prosperous and successful by meditating on the Word day and night. This principle is essential not only to ensure we improve our understanding of God's Word but also to ensure that our thoughts are in order. We have to maintain our focus on what God has to say concerning our lives.

One of the reasons it is so vital to renew our minds daily with the Word of God is because the enemy is always attempting to influence our thinking. We have to be careful not to fall into the trap of doubting God at any given time. It is imperative to close the door to negativity and confusion. As people of God, we are meant to live victoriously.

We have a responsibility to broaden our capacity to receive wisdom and understanding from God. He trusts the keen listener to carry out His instructions precisely as He stated without wavering. As you spend more time meditating on the Word, your thoughts will become more positive, and your actions will follow suit. You will know without a doubt when God is speaking to you through His Word. That is because you will have invested ample time focusing on what is written in the scriptures.

When you study God's Word and seek to understand Him, it will be difficult to make the mistake of not knowing what He is saying to you concerning your life. You just have to decide to believe what God said and refuse to let outside influences cause you to doubt Him.

Confusion should never exist in the mind of a person who takes time to observe and focus on what God has spoken concerning his or her life. God's Word reveals truth, clarity, and understanding. This is extremely important because we get discouraged too often after it appears that things are not going as planned. When you face a situation that challenges what God said, remember that His Word will never return void.

Isaiah 55: 10-11 (NKJV) says, "For as the rain comes down, and the snow from heaven, and do not return here, But water the earth, and make it bring forth and bud, that it may give seed to the sower and bread to the eater, so shall My word be that goes forth from My mouth; it shall not return to Me void, but it shall accomplish what I please, and it shall prosper in the thing for which I sent it."

As we manage our thoughts, we also have to learn to recognize and overcome potential obstacles. Applying what we have learned from the Word is vital. For instance, if fear is one of your vulnerable areas, find every scripture that promises you the opposite of fear—courage, strength, and victory. Speak those promises over your life every time fear attempts to come your way.

Next, pay attention to the enemy's strategies. Find the root cause of negative thoughts and counter them with the Word of God. The more you practice using God's Word, the more skillful you will become. It takes discipline to eliminate old thought patterns and allow God to renew your mind. However, it is a key to enjoying the peace of mind He intended for us. Every day you awaken is a new opportunity to study and learn more about what God has in store for your life.

You can create the unimaginable. God will bring change into your life and get you well on your way to unlocking your potential if you choose to meditate on His Word consistently. It will preserve you and strengthen your awareness of upcoming challenges. It will also guide you in making decisions that will continue to keep you on the path to your divine destiny.

Positive Thinking

Philippians 4: 8 (AMP) says, "For the rest, brethren, whatever is true, whatever is worthy of reverence and is honorable and seemly, whatever is just, whatever is pure, whatever is lovely and lovable, whatever is kind and winsome and gracious if there is any virtue and excellence, if there is anything worthy of praise, think on and weigh and take account of these things—fix your minds on them."

If you were to recall some negative thoughts that recently crossed your mind and decided to challenge them with God's Word, you would notice that there is at least one positive thought that can supersede each negative thought. For example, you might have experienced some disappointment or a missed opportunity, but the Bible says all things are working together for your good (see Romans 8:28).

The next time you find yourself thinking about something negative, challenge those thoughts with what God's Word says in Philippians 4:8. Whatever the negative message or perception is, ask these questions:

Is it…

…true?

There is a difference between fact and truth. For example, a fact could be that you didn't accomplish a goal as planned. The truth, however, says, "Delight yourself also in the Lord, and He will give you the desires and secret petitions of your heart" (Psalm 37:4,

AMP). Revisit your goal and see it from the perspective of God's promise.

...worthy of reverence, honorable, and seemly? Do your thoughts uplift and praise God?

If not, what can you do to bring honor to Him? Psalm 69: 30-31 (KJV) says, "I will praise the name of God with a song and will magnify Him with thanksgiving, and it will please the Lord ..."

...just?

To think about what is just, there has to be the possibility that you faced an unjust situation. Has God given you victory in a situation lately? Has He avenged you of an adversary? Your thoughts of how just and righteous God is and how He has defended you in so many instances should be an encouragement. Realize that if He did it before, He will do it again.

...pure?

Purity comes without a tainted motive or hidden agenda. God's motives for your life are pure. He wants what is best for you. No matter what your present circumstances look like, the truth is He wants you to walk in the victory He ordained for you from the beginning of time. He desires for you to assume your rightful place in the kingdom.

...lovely and loveable?

God's love for you is all you need to enjoy a lifetime of peace, joy, and happiness. We do not remind ourselves often enough just how much He loves us. We tend to make the mistake of connecting what we see with how we think God feels about us. But if it doesn't line up with what He said in His Word, it isn't accurate. His thoughts toward us are filled with goodness and love.

...kind, winsome, and gracious?

The simple fact that you woke up this morning indicates God's grace continues to cover you. When you least deserve it, His grace covers you. Where would you be right now if it had not been for God, who is on your side? He has always been here, fighting your battles and seeing you through to the end, day after day, night after night. Where would you be right now if it had not been for God, who took care of you when you didn't know how to take care of yourself? What would you have done had He not rescued you from the traps of the enemy? He has been kind, winsome, and gracious to us all.

...virtuous, excellent, and worthy of praise?

We can sum this description up in one word—God. He is all of these things and so much more! Your life is evidence of the manifestation of God's excellence. He is worthy of all praise. We should count it an honor to be able to give Him glory. Not everyone has the mind or the desire to praise Him. It is a privilege to have such an experience.

As we reflect on the positive things available to us and compare them to the negative thoughts that try to invade our minds, there is no doubt that good always outweighs bad. God's awesome power, everlasting love, and magnificent splendor far exceed any problem we think we might have. He is so much more valuable than our negative situations. Remember this every time the enemy tries to bring negativity your way.

God is bigger than your problems. Let Him take His rightful place in your mind by exalting Him above every other thought. Praise Him by placing Him above your worries. Every time you lift the name of Jesus, you are removing negative thoughts. Continue to manage your thoughts by focusing on God and all He represents.

CHAPTER 6 SUMMARY

What are some ways that you can begin to overcome some of the distractions in your life?

What does it mean to meditate on God's Word?

Why is meditation on God's Word vital to your success?

In what ways does positive thinking help you and those around you?

Thoughts for Reflection

CHAPTER 7

Develop an A-W-E-S-O-M-E
Prayer Life

After studying the scriptures, listening to various teachings, and reading several books on how to pray, I have concluded that the most effective way to pray is from the heart. The Bible tells us that God knows our thoughts from afar. In other words, He already knows what we want to say to Him before we even think about it ourselves. Reaching God through prayer should never feel like a task. Instead, it is a joyful experience that draws us closer to Him. Even so, our God is a God of order. Jesus established a pattern of prayer for us to follow.

After this manner, therefore, pray ye: Our Father which art in heaven, Hallowed be thy name. Thy kingdom come, Thy will be done in earth, as it is in heaven. Give us this day our daily bread. And forgive us our debts, as we forgive our debtors. And lead us not into temptation, but deliver us from evil: For thine is the kingdom and the power, and the glory, forever. Amen (Matthew 6: 9-13, KJV).

This pattern of prayer consists of seven major parts. This is significant because the number seven is God's perfect number. It signifies completion and wholeness. When referring to these seven parts, I use the acronym AWESOME as a reference point. As we pray, we can always expect something awesome to take place.

The seven parts to the pattern of prayer are to **acknowledge, worship, expect, sustain, omit, monitor,** and **establish.**

Acknowledge: *"Our Father which art in heaven"*

Acknowledging that God is our father is the foundation for our relationship with Him. This means not only is He powerful, all-knowing, and all-seeing, He is our Father. His DNA is within us. Thus, we should have confidence in knowing that no matter what we need, He will provide. Moreover, everything that is in the Father is also within us.

Knowing God is our Heavenly Father, we can be sure of several things. First, we can't hide anything from Him. We don't have to be ashamed to go to Him at any given time and talk to Him about what is in our hearts. No matter how embarrassing, complicated, or difficult it may seem, God already knows everything there is to know about us.

He is always available to us. We don't have to make an appointment to enter into His presence. We can talk to Him any time. He is approachable and enjoys fellowship with His children. He wants us to draw near to Him.

Worship: *"Hallowed be thy name"*

Being in the presence of God motivates us to express how we feel toward Him. As we acknowledge Him for who He is in our lives, we begin to express our gratitude in the form of worship. We render the utmost respect, love, and adoration to Him because He is God Almighty.

We declare He is Alpha and Omega, the beginning and the end. He is the first and the last; besides Him there is no other. He seeks true worshippers—those who will worship in spirit and in truth.

John 4:23-24 (NKJV) says, "But the hour is coming, and now is, when the true worshipers will worship the

Father in spirit and truth; for the Father is seeking such to worship Him. God is Spirit, and those who worship Him must worship in spirit and truth."

An important thing to remember about worship is that it does not take place just during prayer. It is a lifestyle. Worship is what we do to uplift the name of God—not just what we say. Our hearts transform when we exalt God. No longer are we concentrating on our problems. We surrender everything to Him and focus on uplifting Him. As we enter into true worship, the presence of God manifests itself—God shows up on the scene. Fear then turns into faith. Sadness turns into joy. Hopelessness becomes hopefulness.

Weeping turns into laughter. Suddenly, you know the answer is on its way.

Expect: *"Thy kingdom come, Thy will be done in earth, as it is in heaven."*

Praying, "thy kingdom come" implies that some aspect God's kingdom has yet to be made manifest in our lives. The "kingdom of God" is His way of doing things. Each time we pray, we should ask that He align our lives with His way of doing things, and to set in order everything that is out of place. This includes our thoughts, actions, behavior, and circumstances that are beyond our control. Every aspect of our lives must be in accordance with the kingdom of God. In other words, when we pray, we want God to have His way.

Praying for God's will means that things might not necessarily happen the way we initially thought they should. Many people have a problem with this part of the payer. It requires total trust in God and the belief that He knows what is best. It is human tendency to think differently from God. We focus on the here and now; meanwhile, God has already seen the outcome. We can only see what is directly in front of us. Yet, God knows what is around the corner. Sometimes, our lives can be like mazes; there are so many twists and turns we can make. We might not know whether to look left or right, but if we look to God, He will guide us straight along the path He intends for us to take. Psalm 24:7 (KJV) says, "Lift up your heads, O ye gates; even lift them up ye everlasting doors and the King of glory shall come in." If you want God to come into your situations, don't focus all of your attention at what is going on in front of you. Look toward heaven instead."

Sustain: *"Give us this day our daily bread"*

When we pray, we are to ask God for daily sustenance. Notice, however, that we are not just asking for ourselves. As the scriptures don't say, "My" father, which art in heaven, they also don't say "my" daily bread. Instead, we ask for "our" daily bread. This is important to note because God's gifts are meant to be shared with others. This includes our time, talent, treasure, knowledge, and wisdom. They are not just your gifts—they are for everyone.

Our daily bread is a necessity we cannot afford to live without. As mentioned earlier, we need the Word of God to sustain us. Just as we will get sick and eventually die of starvation if we don't eat physical food, we will die spiritually if we don't have the Word of God. It is what keeps us balanced and results in our spiritual growth.

Omit: *"And forgive us our debts, as we forgive our debtors"*

We all have faults we prefer not to mention. When we approach God in prayer, we ask for His forgiveness or dismissal of all the wrong we have committed. We need God to look past our sins and see the blood of Jesus, which has spoken for our sins. We also agree to forgive wrongs that others have done against us. This is often a painful process for many. We don't always have the same attitude toward other people that God has toward us. Sometimes, our natural tendency is to hold grudges. We can think of many reasons why it is hard to forgive those who have offended us. Yet, to continue moving forward, we have to forfeit whatever right we believe we have to judge or criticize another person for his or her offenses.

This is true regardless of whether or not the person asks us for forgiveness. Most of the time, they will not. Forgiving others is more of a benefit to us than it is to the ones who offend us. It cleanses our hearts and minds and helps us mature spiritually. Colossians 3:13 (AMP) says, "Be gentle and forbearing with one another, and if one has a difference against another, readily pardoning each other; even as the Lord has forgiven you, so must you also."

Monitor: *"And lead us not into temptation, but deliver us from evil"*

We need God to monitor our walk continuously to ensure we don't fall into the traps the enemy puts in our way. God knows the path we are traveling and is the only One who sees what is ahead. Therefore, we must rely on Him to lead us away from the enemy's snares. Any time we are tempted with something that opposes God, it is there to deceive us and cause us to fall. When we ask God to deliver us, however, we are inviting Him to provide us with insight and wisdom that will keep us from falling.

Establish: *"For thine is the kingdom, and the power, and the glory, forever. Amen."*

We conclude our prayer by reaffirming that God is sovereign over all our situations and that all power belongs to Him. Furthermore, all of the honor and glory for the victory, which results from our prayer belongs to Him. The matter is then established and settled in a secure position—it is in His hands.

Remove the "if" from your heart

Have you ever noticed times when God answered some of your prayers almost immediately, while some other prayers seemingly go unanswered? We know God never changes and that His way is perfect. It is not that He wants to answer some of our prayers but not others.

One reason we have this experience is that when we go to God, He does not hear what comes from our lips—He hears what comes from our hearts. Sometimes we say one thing with our mouths, but our hearts are actually saying something else.

One day I was getting ready to go to a class, and as I was preparing to exit my car, I realized I had forgotten to tell my husband something very important. I had attempted several times to call him on my mobile phone, but with poor reception in that particular area near my class, the call would not go through. After a moment of hesitation, I just quietly whispered, "Father, I need to get in touch with him!" I dialed the number again. Instantly, the call went through successfully. I thought to myself, "Wow! I wonder how that happened." There was something about the way it all happened that let me know it was no coincidence. In fact, I'd often tried making calls from that same area several times thereafter and was not able to get a call through.

As the years went by and my relationship with the Lord developed, I continued to wonder about that moment. What was different about the way I prayed? My words were few. I was not in a state of panic or desperation. What really happened that day?

Sometimes when we pray, we have no confidence that God will actually do what we are asking of Him. Instead of releasing our faith, we tempt Him. In other words, our lips are saying, "God I know that according to your word, you will bring it to pass. Your Word says this, and I believe it to be so." While our lips are saying one thing, our hearts are saying something else. Something such as, "If you really are God, please do this for me." Then, when the "if" is not satisfied, we become depressed, weary, confused, and frustrated. You wonder how He can do this but not that, and why it always seems that when you ask for just one thing, He does not seem to hear you. Remember, the enemy tried using this tactic (yes, it is a tactic) when Jesus was in the wilderness: "If thou be the Son of God, command that these stones be made bread," (Matthew 4:3).

As children of God, we don't need to use tactics to have our prayers answered. Instead, we must activate our confidence in Him. We don't have to wait to see if He will answer us. We know He will answer us. We don't have to question His existence, supremacy, or His love for us. We already know He is the King of kings and the Lord of lords. When God's Word promises us something, the matter is settled. Therefore, always go to Him with confidence. Remember, regardless of what is coming from your lips, God is listening to your heart. What is your heart saying today?

Wait Patiently

Another reason it might appear as though God has not answered some of our prayers when we expect is simply that we need to be more patient. God uses His Word to develop our character as we wait patiently and allow His Word to settle in our hearts.

For example, suppose you have been praying for God to change a situation in your life. Not long after you pray, you happen to hear a message that encourages you not to worry. As a result of hearing the message, you might decide to meditate on Bible verses that emphasize peace and the need to cast all of your cares on God. Before seeing an immediate change to your situation, however, you might begin to experience challenges instead. The challenges cause you to practice what you have learned about not worrying. As you continue facing obstacles and applying biblical principles directly to your circumstances, you gain more inner strength and develop new habits that improve your life. You attain small victories along the way to receiving answers to your prayers.

When going through the process of waiting, it might appear that God has ignored or forgotten your requests. You can rest assured that He is well aware of your concerns and He will answer you at an appointed time. While you are waiting, allow God to develop other areas of your life. They all work together for your good in the end. Seek Him for guidance and encouragement. Put His principles into practice, so that at the appointed time, you will not only receive the answers to your prayers, but you will also have greater wisdom, a deeper level of understanding, and more patience.

Understanding Opposites

The enemy will try to make you focus on the opposite of the truth that God has declared for your life. Every negative issue you face is the opposite of what God has in store for you. For example, if you are struggling financially, it is because you are supposed to be walking in an abundance of finances.

Your opponent, the enemy, tries to distract you with problematic things that are the exact opposite of what God has in store for your life. Rather than focusing on the adversity, remember God has a great plan for you. He does not want you to worry. Instead, trust in Him and lean on His Word. Allow God to give you peace even in the midst of trouble. You will receive what God promised you!

I learned this principle after struggling with letting go of the past. The harder I tried to let go, the more reminders of the past seemed to be in my way. For a while, I asked God to remove my pain, but as time passed by, the problem only seemed to grow worse.

One day, while attending a church service with one of my relatives, I went to the altar for prayer, and the pastor said to me, "Your worst days are behind you and the best is yet to come." I considered what the pastor said, and was encouraged over those inspiring words for a short while. But the problem did not disappear automatically.

Then, when I was at another church, another minister said almost the exact same thing to me: "Everything that happened before you walked through that door is behind you. Your worst days are over and the best is yet to come." Once again, I was moved. I was surprised that the same words were spoken to me. I knew it was not a coincidence. But still, the problem persisted.

Then later, the Holy Spirit spoke to me from within: "The reason you've had such a difficult time letting go of your past is because you have an awesome future." The intensity of your tribulation tells you two things: the victory waiting for you is even greater than your former problems and there are others who can benefit from your testimony.

You might meet people and have the opportunity to share your deliverance experience with them, or you might end up praying for them as the Holy Spirit leads you. God will often do the work in others without your knowledge of it. Often when He does things for people, they don't know that intercessory prayer played an instrumental part in the whole process.

Friend or Foe?

Another interesting thing about opposites is that people we consider friends are often enemies, while those we think are enemies, are actually our friends. When we pray for our friends, according to the Word of God, we open up the door to receive the same blessing that God bestowed on Job. Job 42:10 (KJV) says, "And the Lord turned the captivity of Job and restored his fortunes when he prayed for his friends; also the Lord gave Job twice as much as he had before."

The ones whom God referred to as Job's friends— Eliphaz, Bildad, and Zophar were those who insulted him and criticized him harshly. They tormented him and broke him down with their words. You might be saying, "That doesn't sound like anyone I would call a friend."

What Job's friends did not know, however, is that by adding to Job's affliction, they were actually pushing him closer to God. Thus, they set him up to receive more than he ever had before in his life. This was contingent upon Job's willingness to show compassion for his friends by praying that God would grant them mercy.

Another example is found when Jesus, knowing that Judas was betraying him, referred to Judas as his friend (See Matthew 26:50). Judas' actions, which were intended to harm Jesus, had actually assisted him in getting to the cross, where ultimately the will of the Father would be completed. In the midst of being crucified, Jesus prayed, "Father, forgive them, for they know not what they do" (Luke 23:34, KJV).

Why is it important to pray for those who mean you harm? Because Luke 17:2 (KJV) says, "It would be more profitable for him if a millstone were hung around his neck and he were hurled into the sea ..."

In Romans 8:28, God promises that all things work together for good for those who love Him. He also promises in Isaiah 54:17 that no weapon formed against you will prosper. Even so, your ability to show mercy toward those, who mean you harm further demonstrates the qualities that God has placed within you.

Why is the reward so great when you pray for God to have mercy on those who meant to hurt you? Because praying such a prayer with sincerity and truthfulness, is only possible when you have matured to a level of wisdom and understanding in God that has allowed you to respond this way. At this point, you are more concerned with completing God's work and His will in your life than you are with getting revenge.

In this way, you announce to all of heaven that you are no longer standing in the way; that God is supreme and He reigns in your life. You surrender your will and crucify your own flesh, thereby releasing God to move in your life in the manner that He pleases.

"Confess your faults one to another, and pray one for another, that ye may be healed. The effectual fervent prayer of a righteous man availeth much," (James 5:16, KJV).

CHAPTER 7 SUMMARY

Describe a specific event that took place in your life where prayer was the key to a positive outcome.

What are some of the benefits to prayer?

What would happen if we didn't pray on a regular basis?

Why should we make it a habit to pray for our friends?

Thoughts for Reflection

CHAPTER 8

Practice Discipline
and Diligence

God rewards diligence. It demonstrates that you care enough about something to put forth more than the minimum required effort toward achieving it. Diligent people don't have time to complain or make up excuses for why they have not reached their goals. They don't look for other people to blame for their failures. Instead, they take their mistakes and pitfalls and turn them into lessons learned. Diligence and discipline go hand in hand for various reasons. You cannot have one without the other.

It takes discipline to be diligent, and it takes diligence to build and maintain a life of discipline and order. Diligence and discipline inspire change for the better within your life. As one who has been called into the Kingdom, you will always be moving forward to different levels of faith, assignment, and victory. As such, there is a great deal of work to be done, which requires much spiritual preparation. You can't afford to waste time on situations that hinder your progress.

A diligent lifestyle makes it easier to pass the tests and trials that we as believers will encounter. No matter who you are, there is one thing you'll never be able to avoid in life—the need to be tested. You might wonder why anyone would view testing as a need. The answer is simple. Tests are necessary because they reveal what you need to know about yourself. As believers, there are different types of tests we must undergo. Let's look at some examples.

Assessments

An assessment is usually a compilation of several tests, in which each test measures a different area. When designed correctly, they provide an accurate picture of how you measure up. Usually, when you are assessed, an upgrade or a new assignment of some type is underway. For students, assessments of academic performance often determine whether they will pass on to the next higher grade. Some professions require candidates to take assessments and achieve a certain score before they are qualified to work within that profession. As a believer, you can expect assessments to occur regularly. This is where you find out how much of God's Word you have actually allowed to really settle in your heart and become part of your life.

Unlike man-made assessments, God's tests are always open-book. In other words, you can always go back to the Word of God to find the solution to what you are experiencing. To pass, however, you have to apply the Word directly to your situation. No one likes to be tested. It can be a very difficult, frustrating time in a person's life. If you try to avoid your tests, however, you won't make much progress. To get through the test with the least amount of pain, you need to practice diligence and discipline. The more you practice applying God's Word to your life each day, the less painful an experience you will have when you're tested.

The Fitness Test

From a physical perspective, fitness tests show us how in shape we are due to regular exercise and proper nutrition. In the Army, for example, everyone must complete and pass a weigh-in along with a physical fitness test. This is because when preparing for battle, your weight cannot be so excessive that it slows you down and puts you at risk for being wounded or killed in combat.

Some fitness tests may consist of a variety of exercises, such as push-ups, sit-ups, and two-mile endurance run. Push-ups are typically designed to improve one's upper-body strength. Although understanding the concept of a push-up is quite simple, doing a certain number within a specified time is not easy unless you exercise regularly. If you exercise to a point where you become able to do more than what is required, the test will not be as difficult as it would be if you did not exercise regularly at all. If you cheat yourself during exercise sessions, neglect to use the proper form when doing push-ups, and fail to do the required number of repetitions, you will be at risk of pain and injury when it is time to take the test. In fact, depending on how undisciplined you were during your training sessions, you could end up failing the test.

From a spiritual perspective, many people refer to PUSH in terms of an acronym for Pray Until Something Happens. In other words, the spiritual push-up test measures your persistence in prayer. You might start out with one specific prayer request that you are waiting for God to answer. Once you see the principles in God's Word actually beginning to work for your life, and God answers that first request, you will rejoice. You should not stop there, however. This is just the beginning of a lifelong faith walk.

Just as with the physical push-up, the more diligent and consistent your prayer life becomes, the less difficult it will become to release your worries and exercise your faith. If you only pray every once in a while, or if you don't take your prayers seriously, you will not withstand the tests and trying of your faith. Indeed, you will find yourself at the same level of faith until you decide to make a change and establish a more disciplined prayer life.

From the perspective of exercise, sit-ups improve one's abdominal strength. From a spiritual perspective, we can use SIT-UP as an acronym for Stay in Tune - Uncompromising Persistence. In this sense, the spiritual sit-up test is designed to measure how well we rise from adverse circumstances.

Some fitness experts say the sit-up exercise can have a tendency to put too much strain on the back and recommend doing other exercises to achieve the same or better results. I agree with this opinion, from both a natural and a spiritual perspective. You don't need an adverse situation (that is, you don't need to be flat on your back) to find out how in-tune you are with the Holy Spirit or to determine how steadfast and persistent you are. In other words, you don't have to be in a position of defeat to discover how much inner strength you possess. Sometimes, you can find yourself going from one level of victory to the next. Preparing for these changes requires just as much strength as going from defeat to victory.

An endurance run measures one's ability to start and complete a particular distance within a specified length of time. Weight plays an important role in this area, because with practice, the less weight you have to carry, the easier this test will become. Hebrews 12:1 (AMP) says we are to "… strip off and throw aside every unnecessary weight and that sin which so readily clings to and entangles us, and let us run with patient endurance and steady active persistence the appointed course of the race that is set before us."

Both the physical and spiritual run measures the runner's endurance. To prepare for this test from a spiritual perspective, you have to practice consistency. In other words, don't start something and quit prematurely because things are not working the way you think they should. Endure whatever challenges you have to endure, but don't ever give up. If you start a regular prayer and study schedule, you can automatically expect distractions to start trying to get in the way. But, don't allow the distractions or anything else to stop you from continuing that schedule. Even if you have to reschedule for a different time on the same day, make the adjustment. Just don't give up.

When Tested, Go the Distance

In the movie "Secretariat" (based on a true story), a prize horse gained a great deal of attention for his ability to run at record-breaking speed. His endurance was questionable, however, because he had not been put to the test when it came to running long distances. When the time finally came for him to run a major race at a distance he had never experienced, many people were concerned. The skeptics said no one knows what his true ability is. But his owner's response was that Secretariat knew his limits and she encouraged him to run his race.

When the day came for the much-anticipated race, Secretariat took off and ran at an unusual speed. Typically, he started off slowly and gained momentum as the race progressed, but not this time. He started off faster than usual. For that reason, people really began to worry that he would give out too soon and lose the race for sure. Surprisingly, the further he ran, the faster he became. His ability was unbelievable, and it astonished the entire crowd of people who watched him cross the finish line. Winning by 31 lengths, Secretariat had set a new world record.

When you are put to the test and are unsure of how things will pan out, don't be afraid to give it all you have. The results could amaze you and everyone else around you. Remember that with God, all things are possible. There may be times when your challenges seem to be more than you bargained for, but just remember whose you are. You have God's ability within you. Use what He gave you to run your race and believe that nothing shall be impossible for you.

CHAPTER 8 SUMMARY

What can you do differently in your own life to improve your level of diligence?

How do diligence and discipline go hand in hand?

In what ways has God rewarded you for diligently seeking His face?

What happens when we go through tests and do not apply what we have learned from them?

Thoughts for Reflection

CHAPTER 9

Maintain Your God-Given Authority

The Word declares that we are more than conquerors through Christ Jesus. A conqueror is someone who can triumph over obstacles or opposition. To be more than a conqueror means your wins are over the top! Through Jesus, you can stand firm in a place of continuous victory. Keep in mind that this is despite the way things look on the outside. As mentioned earlier, this doesn't mean negative situations won't occur in your life. However, what it does mean is that when things do happen, as long as you maintain your position in Christ, He will use your situations to benefit you down the road – if you are willing to let Him use you in that way.

Disappointments are inevitable. They happen to everyone at some point, whether on a small or large scale. If you listen closely and keep the lines of communication open with God, you will see that with each disappointment comes a valuable lesson to be learned somewhere in the middle of the situation. To implement God's authority in your life successfully, you must fully understand how to maintain your posture as "more than a conqueror."

Ephesians 6:10-18 (KJV) says, "Finally, my brethren, be strong in the Lord, and in the power of his might. Put on the whole armor of God that ye may be able to stand against the wiles of the devil. For we wrestle not against flesh and blood, but against principalities, against powers, against the rulers of the darkness of this world, against spiritual wickedness in high places.

Wherefore take unto you the whole armor of God, that ye may be able to withstand in the evil day, and having done all, to stand. Stand therefore, having your loins girt about with truth, and having on the breastplate of righteousness; and your feet shod with the preparation of the gospel of peace; above all, taking the shield of faith, wherewith ye shall be able to quench all the fiery darts of the wicked. And take the helmet of salvation, and the sword of the Spirit, which is the Word of God: Praying always with all prayer and supplication in the Spirit, and watching thereunto with all perseverance and supplication for all saints."

In this passage of scripture, the Apostle Paul takes time to explain that it is necessary to arm ourselves properly with God's whole armor. Sometimes, when opposition arises, we miss the lesson because we are too busy looking at the wrong thing. What we are up against is often more serious than something like an envious person or someone who wants to hold us back. Usually, the opposition we face is from one of the four levels Paul mentions—principalities, powers, rulers of darkness, or spiritual wickedness in high places. Resistance occurs in many forms, but know that there is always a strategy—not a very brilliant one, but a strategy nonetheless.

Stand Firm

The purpose of a wrestling match is to get a hold over one's opponent and ultimately take them down. That is what the enemy wants to do with you, especially when you are on the verge of something that will impact the Kingdom of Heaven in a positive and significant way. So, for the enemy to wrestle you down, he uses what the Bible refers to as wiles—deceit and trickery.

Part of avoiding the enemy's deceit is to pay attention to what is happening. Know what the enemy does to deceive you. In Genesis, God told Eve that she and her offspring would be bruised in the heel by the enemy.

While we are the biological offspring of Eve, we are God's spiritual offspring through Christ Jesus. Any time we step out of our place and begin walking in carnality, we subject ourselves to being bruised in the heel.

The feet represent authority; to stand in the biblical context means to proclaim officially. So, when your enemy attempts to bruise your heel, it means he is trying to trip you up and cause you to stumble out of your place of authority – the authority that is only valid as long as you remain in Christ. Once you become aware of how the enemy tries to trip you up, the next step is to determine your weak areas.

What makes you lose your focus? What gets your blood boiling? Why? What makes you angry? What makes you happy? What causes you to become sad? What drives you to lose sleep at night? Pause and think about these things for a moment. The enemy will try to use these things against you every time. Why attack someone in an area in which they are healthy? That would make no sense at all. Knowing this, the next important thing to note is that in Matthew 12:25, Jesus stated that a kingdom divided against itself will not stand. We need to connect with other believers upon whom we can call to pray with us and vice versa.

Just as the enemy has strategic lines of opposition, you need to have a strong force of believers filled with the Holy Spirit with whom you can connect for fasting, prayer, studying the Word, and encouragement.

As you strengthen your walk with Christ, you will also enhance your level of wisdom and discernment regarding people. God is there to direct you and to help you choose your connections wisely.

Wear Your Armor

There are several things we are told our whole armor includes. The first is the belt of truth (See Ephesians 6:14). The truth of God's Word must always remain at the forefront of our minds. We must surround ourselves with it and ignore every lie from the enemy.

How do you know the difference between the truth and a lie? Study the Word of God. His Word declares in

John 16:13 that the Spirit of Truth (the Holy Ghost) will show you all things. We need the shield of faith. When the lies look more convincing than the truth, we have to believe by faith—we must believe in that which we cannot physically see.

The helmet of salvation keeps our minds in perfect peace (Ephesians 6:17). If the enemy can cause you to doubt that you belong to Christ, he can also cause you to question your authority. The salvation you receive from declaring Jesus your Lord and Savior must be ever-present in your mind.

Contentment

When we balance our lives to the point where we are content on any level, we can exercise God's authority more effectively. This occurs because regardless of what we have or don't have, the enemy will not be able to use things like worldly possessions against us. I have read countless stories of people who became famous and wealthy and started changing for the worse. I have seen reports in the news about how some have lost nearly all their fame and fortune yet continue to lead destructive lives. What happens in these instances?

Their possessions or the lack thereof determine their livelihood, and they stray from God. Some of these people have not yet established their relationships with God.

To maintain our God-given authority, we need to have a solid foundation in Christ—one that is not destroyed when our situations change. Stay closely connected to God and know that our wealth in Him never runs out. If we live being satisfied with where we are in Christ, we'll find that He will strengthen us so that we will be victorious and at peace always.

When Jesus is the center of our lives, we won't allow wealth to rule us. Therefore, we can have great wealth and still get plenty of sleep each night. When God is our focus, finances don't cause us to compromise our integrity. Instead, we look to God for help.

I have learned, in whatsoever state I am, therewith to be content. I know both how to be abased, and I know how to abound: everywhere and in all things, I am instructed both to be full and to be hungry, both to abound and to suffer need. I can do all things through Christ, which strengthens me (Philippians 4:11-13, KJV).

During my previous times of testing, when it looked as if there was no help to be found, reciting Psalm 23 kept me going. It was a constant reminder that I belong to Jesus. I was not just some fly-by-night person who had no covenant. No, I have a Shepherd. I belong to someone. I have been bought with a price! I am His. I encourage you to find a scripture of your own—one that will remind you every day that you belong to Christ. When challenges come, and you don't see any hope or help, you can rest assured that Jesus is your hope and your help. No matter what it looks like on the outside, you have a family—you have a Father, the King of Kings, and the Lord of Lords—your Shepherd is responsible for your well-being. He has given you authority, and He will take care of you.

CHAPTER 9 SUMMARY

What lessons can you take from some of your recent disappointments?

How will those lessons help you to improve the outcome in future situations?

Give one example of how the enemy may have tried to deceive you into believing something opposite of God's Word.

Review Ephesians 6. How do you intend to use your armor to combat the lies of the enemy from now on?

Thoughts for Reflection

CHAPTER 10

Know Him for Yourself

Who Do Men Say That He Is?

When Jesus came into the coasts of Caesarea Philippi, he asked his disciples, "who do men say that I the Son of man am?" And they said some say that thou art John the Baptist: some, Elias; and others, Jeremias, or one of the prophets. (Matthew16:13-14, KJV)

As I thought about that question, I began to consider my personal experiences through my walk with Christ. I could describe who He is to me in many ways, and I felt inspired to share a few of these descriptions:

He who Opens

"I know your works. See, I have set before you an open door, and no one can shut it...." (Revelations 3:8, NKJV).

I used to think this scripture regarding the open door referred to opportunities. One day I was in prayer, and I quoted this scripture. The Holy Spirit then prompted me to close my eyes and visualize a door. As

I saw myself walking through the door, I realized what was through the door was much more than an opportunity. It was access to everything I needed. As I passed through the door, I began to call out things that were there: peace, healing, divine counsel, joy, protection, wisdom. There were no limits! The Lord allowed me to understand that He is the Way that leads to wholeness in every area of our lives. I guarantee that if you reach for God, He will guide you through the open door that no man can shut.

The Composer

During her freshman year of high school, my daughter had to complete a band assignment that consisted of composing sheet music. When creating this music, she had to choose a tempo, which determined the pace of the music. She also had to ensure the melody and harmony were established and that everything flowed well. When I listened to her composition, I was amazed! She had taken the time to develop musical phrases while ensuring the proper range of notes. She had also carefully chosen the right tempo for the song. In my opinion, she created a masterpiece.

This reminds me of how God developed a specific plan for our lives. He created a song and invited us to walk in harmony and syncopation with the beat of His heart. Every time I think about the wonders that He created, I can hear His love singing like a beautifully-created song. When I gaze at the stars, I feel the rhythm of His perfect beat, and I am reminded that His way is perfect. All we have to do is stay connected with Him, walk in harmony with His Word, and keep the rhythm of His perfect plan.

The Finisher

When I reflect on my personal story, I recall several lessons learned in each stage of my life. I also realize that despite every challenge, God has always been faithful. His hand has always extended toward me, as He has waited patiently to pick me up from every fall.

God's presence has hovered over me through days and nights of sadness. He has comforted me when I felt like no one else cared. When I didn't see the point in looking forward to another day, He encouraged me to look up. I experienced times of difficulty in my life that made no sense. Every time I tried to figure out the cause, I never seemed to reach a reasonable conclusion.

Although there is often an absence of immediate answers to the question "why," there is a "However." His name is Jesus. In grammar laws, punctuation marks, such as semi-colons or periods, signify the end of a statement. Then there are times when the subsequent statement begins with the word "however." This one word makes its own introductory announcement. It says regardless of what was stated previously, there is still more to be said about the overall situation. The conclusion has not yet been reached; it is not over.

If you are faced with disappointment in any area of life, know that God still has the final word. Look to Him as the Finisher, and allow Him to be the "However" in your personal story.

"Looking unto Jesus the author and finisher of our faith; who for the joy that was set before him endured the cross, despising the shame, and is set down at the right hand of the throne of God" (Hebrews 12:2).

The Listener

I confide in a small number of family members and close friends from time to time regarding certain things. Sometimes I'm only looking for a listening ear, not necessarily words of advice. Yet even within that small circle of people, there are times when I feel as though even they wouldn't understand.

I have been through it all before on numerous occasions. I have engaged in a conversation about a situation or dilemma, hoping to get closer to the solution. Instead, I ended up feeling worse than I did before. So rather than go through that, I decided to start keeping certain things to myself. After a while, I realized something.

There is only one perfect person in all of creation. He has to know the solution to my problems, no matter how complicated they seem. If I talk to Him, there is no way I can lose. I have to end up on the winning side when my conversation with Him is complete. I have learned to make it a priority in life to go to God first—not last.

One evening I was praying about a situation that caused me to feel weighted down. Toward the beginning of the prayer, I was on the surface of the problem, talking about it little by little. Then half-way through, I began to dig deeper within myself. I pulled out everything from within me and laid it all on the table.

After laying it all out, I became silent, and I heard these words: "I heard you." My heart opened, and as I knelt there and paused, I received the true meaning of what the Holy Spirit had spoken into my heart at that moment.

When he said, "I heard you," it meant that my request had gone before Him and was acknowledged, received, and approved. A few moments later, I began to search the scriptures, and I found confirmation of what was spoken in my heart. This is what I found:

And we are sure of this, that he will listen to us whenever we ask him for anything in line with his will. And if we know he is listening when we talk to him and make our requests, we can be sure that he will answer us (1 John 5:14-15, TLB).

The Forgiver of Sins

It would take a lifetime to describe the many sins of which God has forgiven us. I have learned through my walk with Him that when we sin, He wants us to move toward Him, not away from Him. This is the very time we need to get connected to Him. Only He can bring the healing we need, which allows us to continue walking with Him. As we mature in our walk with Christ, we learn through our experiences to place more value on our relationship and level of closeness with Him.

I once heard a teacher make the following statement: "I don't believe in punishing students. Punishment is for criminals. Instead, I believe in consequences." That statement reminds me that God does not treat us like criminals. Like the teacher in this example, I believe that although God does not treat us like criminals when we sin, He allows us to experience the consequences of our actions. Otherwise, we would never change. But His love for us and His plans for our future will remain.

"As far as the east is from the west, so far hath he removed our transgressions from us" (Psalm 103:12, KJV).

The Resurrection

Whenever I read the story about Lazarus in the book of John 11, I am encouraged to trust in God. Just when everyone thought there was nothing left to do about Lazarus' situation, God once again amazed them with His limitless abilities. He is the answer to everything.

When Martha said, "I know that [Lazarus] will rise again in the resurrection at the last day," she was saying, "The answer will show up eventually." Jesus responded by letting her know that she was in the presence of her answer. He was letting her know He is the I AM. She thought it would happen eventually, but it happened instantly. Jesus did not just have a solution; He Is the solution.

Mary and Martha both longed to see their brother alive. For that to happen, the requirement was that resurrection had to take place. Jesus met the requirement because HE IS what they needed—resurrection. He also wants us to understand that HE IS.

If you're in search of hope, look no further! You are in the presence of hope right now! Whatever you need today, God Is! He is the resurrection. Whatever you need and desire, as long as it lines up with His Word and His will for your life, He Is the requirement for restoring it to you! You shall receive it because He Is!

He saith unto them, But who do you say that I am? (Matthew 16:15, NKJV)

I pray that the contents of this book inspired and encouraged you to invest more time with God. He is the best friend you will ever have. You never have to wonder whether He can be trusted because His track record is flawless.

God will not only meet your expectations, but He will also exceed them. I know this because He does it for me every single day. If you want to experience the best life you have ever known, I encourage you to begin spending more time in prayer and studying the Bible. God leads from the front, and He will direct you every step of the way.

If you do not know Jesus Christ as your Lord and Savior, or if you want to renew your relationship with Him, please pray this prayer out loud:

Dear Heavenly Father, I come to You today, realizing that I need you. I desire to turn away from sin and to live the life You have planned for me. I ask your forgiveness for my sins. I believe Your Son, Jesus Christ, died for my sins, that He rose again with all power in His hands, and that He is the resurrection and the life. I confess that Jesus is Lord. I welcome Jesus into my life and invite Him to become my Lord and Savior, to reign in my heart and mind now and forever. I ask that the Comforter, the Holy Spirit, dwell within me now and for the rest of my life. I pray this prayer Jesus Name. Amen.

Congratulations on your decision to accept Jesus into your life. Know that all of heaven rejoices with you! Placing your life in God's hands is the wisest, most important decision you will ever make. You have just made an investment that God guarantees will yield tremendous returns for you now and throughout eternity.

Although you decided to give your life to Christ, He called you first. Before you were even conceived, God had a specific plan for your life. Moreover, you can only fulfill this plan by walking with Him and living the kind of life that pleases Him. Today is the first day of new beginnings.

I pray you will allow the Holy Spirit to lead you to a good church home where the Word of God is going forth with clarity and understanding and where the leadership and church family have hearts, minds, and intentions to do God's will and walk in His way. I ask that you pray and ask the Holy Spirit to lead you to that family—the one that He has for you. I wish you the best in all of your endeavors as you go forth and accomplish all that God has in store for you. God bless you!

CHAPTER 10 SUMMARY

What recent experiences have you encountered and saw God as a (1) He who opens, (2) the Composer, or (3) the Finisher?

Keeping in mind that God hears you and will answer you when you pray, how do you now intend to address those seemingly impossible situations you've been facing?

Knowing that God has forgiven you for past sins, do you now commit to forgiving yourself?

List a problem that needs God's immediate attention. Knowing that He is your present help, trust, and believe He is answering you right now.

Thoughts for Reflection

Made in the USA
Columbia, SC
04 April 2021

35630742R00086